WELCOME TO UNSO

WHAT THIS IS:

Somewhere between planner and journal, *Unsolicited Advice* is a tiny voice in your head that says "Hey, what if???" and helps you keep up with daily written check-ins that might actually change your life. Or just remember what day it is. Or both.

WHAT THIS IS NOT:

Unsolicited Advice isn't a fancy planner that will make you feel bad about being imperfect. I mean, look at my handwriting. It's more about showing up exactly as you are, whenever you can, to reflect on life in your own way. If you miss a week, just catch back up, or start fresh. Without dates, you're in control.

Start on January 1st, or March 9th, or any time, on any day. A new year starts whenever you start counting. Let's go!

TODAY'S DATE:

tarcherperigee

an imprint of Penguin Random House LLC
penguinrandomhouse.com

Most TarcherPerigee books are available at special quantity discounts for bulk
purchase for sales promotions, premiums, fund-raising, and educational needs.
Special books or book excerpts also can be created to fit specific needs. For details,
write: SpecialMarkets@penguinrandomhouse.com.

ISBN 9780593543498

Printed in China
10 9 8 7 6 5 4 3 2 1

Book design by Adam J. Kurtz

Undated 52-Week Planner

ADAM J. KURTZ

UNSOLICITED ADVICE

Bestselling author of 1 Page AT A TIME creative journal

HOW TO USE THIS PLANNER

Can you be completely honest with yourself in these pages? Can you dedicate time to checking in every day, or promise to catch up every few days? Will you make this your own?

Weekly spreads are undated so you can fill in the month and date as you go. If you disappear for a month, just pick right back up. There are monthly sticker tabs in the back; just fold them over the edge of your paper (make sure they stick out a little) to add a tiny bit of structure as the year progresses.

THIS PLANNER ISN'T ABOUT YOU "PERFORMING," BEING OK, OR ON A PATH. IT'S ABOUT KNOWING THE WAY FORWARD SPLINTERS OFF IN MYRIAD DIRECTIONS — ENDLESS DOORWAYS — AND LEAVING A TRAIL BACK THROUGH FEELINGS FELT AND LESSONS LEARNED IN YOUR PERSONAL JOURNEY ON EARTH.

OKAY YIKES, BUT FOR REAL THOUGH.

WRITING THINGS DOWN CAN HELP YOU THINK MORE CLEARLY ABOUT HOW YOU'RE REALLY FEELING.

I type on screens all the time. But when I give myself a few minutes to write, by hand, on paper? That's when my brain has to slow down, long enough to form letters with a pencil, and actually think ~~straight~~ a little more clearly.

Unsolicited Advice is designed to be a space for you to slow down and think, one day at a time, about what's going on.

WE'LL START BY REFLECTING ON THE PREVIOUS 365 DAYS OF YOUR LIFE.

If you're someone who sets up a new planner in advance, this could be in anticipation of January 1st. If you're someone like me, it's probably January 3rd and you're starting out slowly.

We'll start whenever you're ready. Are you about to enter an exciting next chapter of your life? Are you beginning a new project and want to document your progress? Are you hungry for something new? No matter what or when, just choosing to be here for a fresh start counts. Change starts with intention, and I'm intent on both of us thriving this year.

LET'S GET THIS OUT OF THE WAY

I am not "normal." At this point in life it feels too late for me (already weird oops) and also, I no longer believe that normal exists. I'm "too obvious" or "too sentimental" or whatever, and maybe you are too and that's what brought you here.

I'M LITERALLY JUST SOME GUY, WHICH MAKES THIS WHOLE THING UNSOLICITED

However you arrived, you're here now, and we're about to spend a year together. Mostly I'm a tiny voice cheering you on and encouraging you to think about something in a new way every now and then. And for whatever reason, it works.

People have been telling me for years that this is the only planner they've stuck with. That (like me) their planner was becoming a daily "micro-journal" that felt manageable and didn't make them feel guilty or bad about themselves. Slowly, the planner became what it is now—a slightly existential companion unbound by time but united in a specific blend of backhanded optimism, realistic hope, and an occasional jaded streak that sometimes helps keep this thing grounded.

LISTEN, THIS ISN'T FOR EVERYONE. I MEAN ... OBVIOUSLY HAHAHA.

Unsolicited Advice is its own little community of planner people who found their way here at some point over the last decade and have decided to stay. Which means that while you are doing your thing, filling these pages with your personal experience, there are others along on the journey.

THIS CAN BE A MEETING PLACE #NSLCTD

If you ever do feel lonely, you're invited to share a page, a note, or a photo from your world with the hashtag #nslctd ("unsolicited" without vowels). Hopefully the hashtag is unique enough that we'll be the only people following, like a secret club of planner people who are just doing their best without the whole pretending to be picture-perfect thing.

The world can be complicated in so many ways, and it is overwhelming to think about how many of us are out here just trying to have a little fun before it's all over. It's my hope that this bundle of paper—essentially—can be a meeting place for all of us in time and space, in all our big and small feelings, right now, and soon, and again years into the future. Mostly, you'll get out of this planner whatever you put in, and I hope you'll feel able to be as real and open here as possible.

THANK YOU FOR BEING HERE, HAVE A WONDERFUL YEAR, DON'T WORRY WE WILL DEFINITELY TALK ABOUT IT.

WELCOME TO LIFE

YOU
ARE →
HERE*

*FOR NOW

WHERE YOU WANT TO BE:

WHERE YOU ARE NOW:

WHERE YOU'VE BEEN:

REFLECTIONS ON LAST YEAR

Thinking about the last 365 days, what did this past year represent for you?

HIGH POINT LAST YEAR:

Catch me up! What was the highest high or most exciting moment of last year?

IF YOU COULD CHANGE HOW YOU
HANDLED ONE THING LAST YEAR
WHAT WOULD YOU DO DIFFERENTLY?

THE BIGGEST LESSON OF LAST YEAR

What was the major takeaway from last year that might help in the future?*

*YOU CAN'T CHANGE THE PAST BUT YOU CAN CHANGE HOW YOU THINK ABOUT IT...

THE LIST: HOW MANY HAVE YOU DONE?

- [ ] FALL DOWN
- [ ] GET UP
- [ ] RUN AWAY
- [ ] SNORT LAUGH
- [ ] HIGH FIVE
- [ ] SKINNY DIP
- [ ] HAPPY CRY
- [ ] SAD CRY
- [ ] 100 LIKES
- [ ] IMPULSE BUY
- [ ] DAY TRIP
- [ ] FIRST KISS
- [ ] CUDDLE UP
- [ ] FOLLOW BACK
- [ ] BINGE WATCH
- [ ] CHECK IN
- [ ] FREAK OUT
- [ ] CALL HOME
- [ ] SMILE MORE
- [ ] TALK SHIT
- [ ] CHOOSE WISELY
- [ ] DRESS UP
- [ ] F UP
- [ ] LOSE IT

- [ ] LOSE YOURSELF
- [ ] LOSE SOMEONE
- [ ] DIG DEEP
- [ ] DIG IN
- [ ] GO OUT
- [ ] GROW UP
- [ ] READ MORE
- [ ] SELF DISCOVERY
- [ ] CRAVE IT
- [ ] MAKE IT
- [ ] TAKE IT
- [ ] FAKE IT
- [ ] BREAK IT
- [ ] BREAK OUT
- [ ] BREAK AWAY
- [ ] BREAK IN
- [ ] BREAK EVEN
- [ ] SELF LOVE
- [ ] TRUE LOVE
- [ ] LOVE LOVE
- [ ] BAD MOOD
- [ ] BAD BEHAVIOR
- [ ] STOP TIME
- [ ] DISAPPEARING ACT

- ☐ TRY HARDER
- ☐ WONDER WHY
- ☐ FREE REFILL
- ☐ INQUIRE WITHIN
- ☐ NEED MORE
- ☐ WANT MORE
- ☐ GIVE AWAY
- ☐ HELP OUT
- ☐ HELP YOURSELF
- ☐ SET SAIL
- ☐ SET UP
- ☐ STAR GAZE
- ☐ STARRING ROLE
- ☐ DINNER PARTY
- ☐ PART WAYS
- ☐ CREATE CHANGE
- ☐ FEEL LOST
- ☐ FEEL FREE
- ☐ ENJOY IT
- ☐ DÉJÀ VU
- ☐ DÉJÀ VU
- ☐ EYE ROLL
- ☐ BODY ROLL
- ☐ BODY DOUBLE
- ☐ DOUBLE TAP
- ☐ CRY OUT
- ☐ CRY WOLF

- ☐ BE CAREFUL
- ☐ CARE LESS
- ☐ TAKE CARE
- ☐ WALK AWAY
- ☐ DIE INSIDE
- ☐ GO INSIDE
- ☐ SIDE EYE
- ☐ SET ROOTS
- ☐ PLAN AHEAD
- ☐ FEEL SAFE
- ☐ BE GRATEFUL
- ☐ BE HUMBLED
- ☐ JUST BE
- ☐ ALL RIGHT
- ☐ RIGHT ON
- ☐ OPEN DOORS
- ☐ SETTLE UP
- ☐ SETTLE DOWN
- ☐ SLEEP IN
- ☐ SLEEP AWAY
- ☐ FIND OUT
- ☐ FIND JOY
- ☐ FIND YOURSELF
- ☐ FINISH IT
- ☐ FINISH HIM!!
- ☐ DEEP END
- ☐ DEEP BREATH

BIG MOOD

Write, draw, and collage a mood board

that represents your big hopes, goals, or wishes for the next year of your life.

INSTANT GRAMS

Social media can be a great tool for inspiration and connection. Which is also what we're doing in this planner. I've got a full "feed" for you here just in case.

AIRPORT I GUESS	COOL BIRD	GORGEOUS RADIANT SKIN	VOLUMINOUS SHINY HAIRSTYLE
ORANGE (COLOR)	TOP OF THE MORNING	FLAWLESS OUTFIT MOMENT	~~SOMETHING REAL~~ THE BEST VIEW EVER!
HIGHLY CURATED HOME OFFICE	VERY TRENDY SALAD	SMOOTHIE W/ EDIBLE FLOWERS	MUSEUM OF COLORFUL SELFIE BACKDROPS
BLINDED BY THE LIGHT	#TBT TO THE BEST PHOTO OF ME TO EXIST	MAYBE AN ORIGINAL THOUGHT	A NICE TREE
SCREEN-SHOT OF A TWEET	COZY CORNER NOOK	AN ACTUAL MUSEUM WHICH ALSO MUST CATER TO CULTURE	PHOTO OF YOUR PARENT WHEN THEY WERE YOUNG

WHAT HELPS? WHAT DOESN'T?

Think about the resources you have access to. Who or what actually helps you feel better when things aren't going so well? Fill in your circle of care below.

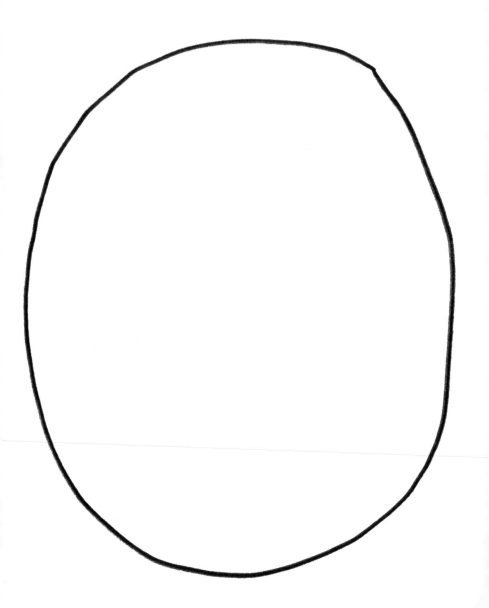

IN THIS MOMENT, HOW DO YOU FEEL ABOUT:

LIFE:

FRIENDS:

FAMILY:

FOOD:

TRAVEL:

DREAMS:

HURT:

GUILT:

STRENGTH:

MEMORY:

LEGEND:

FAITH:

HOPE:

This is all pretty likely to change, so write now and compare again later!

PLANTS:

ART:

GOD:

LOVE:

EVERYTHING:

COMFORT:

EARTH:

TIME:

DEATH:

POP CULTURE:

POLITICS:

SPIRIT:

SELFLESSNESS:

PROJECTIONS FOR THIS YEAR

What might happen? Who will you be? Write now and compare in 365 days.

THE NEXT YEAR OF YOUR
LIFE IS ABOUT TO BEGIN.

CLOSE YOUR EYES, MAKE A
WISH, AND TURN THE PAGE!

HERE
WE
GO
AGAIN

GOALS FOR THE MONTH AHEAD:

SOMETHING TO TRY:

DON'T FORGET:

ONE POSITIVE THOUGHT:

MON   YOU HAVE ~~ALL THE~~ TIME IN THE WORLD

Fill in dates in
whatever format
you like: 1, 1/1,
Jan 1, you get it.

TUES

WED

THURS   WHAT CAN YOU DO FOR SOMEONE ELSE?

SIT UP STRAIGHT   FRI

UNFORTUNATELY YOU ARE RESPONSIBLE??   SAT

                                                          SUN

WEEKLY CHECK-IN: PERSONAL SPACE:

☐ MENTAL HEALTH   Give yourself more of what you need. A scratch
☐ PHYSICAL HEALTH   pad? Reminders? Inspirational quotes? Doodle
☐ _____   area? You'll get a fresh space weekly.
☐ _____
☐ _____   To the left, weekly check-in for health, your
☐ LOOKING FORWARD   own ongoing focus, and generally keeping up!

MON   TAKE CARE OF YOUR PEOPLE

TUES

WED   NOBODY ELSE CAN "FIX" YOU

THURS

ANYTHING CAN ALWAYS HAPPEN   FRI

CAN WE TRY THAT AGAIN?   SAT

                                                    SUN

WEEKLY CHECK-IN: PERSONAL SPACE:

☐ MENTAL HEALTH
☐ PHYSICAL HEALTH
☐ _____
☐ _____
☐ _____
☐ LOOKING FORWARD

THERE'S NO PENALTY
FOR MISSING A
FEW DAYS OF
NOTES OR PLANS.
THERE'S NOBODY
CHECKING UP ON
YOU EXCEPT FOR
YOU— DO WHAT
YOU WANT AND
GROW AT YOUR
OWN PACE.

HOW ARE YOU FEELING TODAY?

RATE YOURSELF ON THE SMILEY SCALE
☺ GOOD   ☺ OKAY   ☹ NOT SO MUCH

○ GENERAL OUTLOOK   ○ PERSONAL GROWTH   ○ PHYSICAL HEALTH

○ PLANNING AHEAD   ○ TAKING CARE   ○ EATING WELL

○ SLEEPING HABITS   ○ BEING AWESOME   ○ MENTAL HEALTH

○ CREATIVE THINKING   ○ SHOWING KINDNESS   ○ CALLING FAMILY

○ WORKING HARD   ○ HAVING FUN   ○ BEING A FRIEND

○ STAYING CALM   ○ TRYING HARD   ○ ENJOYING SPACE

○ EARNING INCOME   ○ GOING OUTSIDE   ○ THAT 1 THING

○ FEELING CONTENT   ○ MAKING CONTENT   ○ FIGURING IT OUT

LIST 10 THINGS YOU'RE HONESTLY GREAT AT:

1.

2.

3.

4.

5.

6.

7.

8.

9. ~~WRITING LISTS~~ THIS 1 JOKE

10.

PICK <u>ONE</u> CONCERN TO FOCUS ON
AND LET'S TRY TO BREAK IT DOWN

FIRST, THE THING

THEN, WHAT IT FEELS LIKE

NEXT, WHAT YOU KNOW AS FACT

NOW, WHAT REQUIRES PATIENCE

I KNOW IT HAPPENED

BUT I FORGET WHAT
IT ACTUALLY FELT LIKE

WHAT'S THE MOST "INSIGNIFICANT"
BUT STILL NOTEWORTHY THING
THAT'S HAPPENED LATELY?

MON   THIS MIGHT BE AN IMPORTANT WEEK

TUES

WED   HAVE A LITTLE FAITH

THURS

OK TIME TO GET SERIOUS   FRI

                                                          SAT

YOU ARE HONESTLY FINE   SUN

WEEKLY CHECK-IN: PERSONAL SPACE:
☐ MENTAL HEALTH
☐ PHYSICAL HEALTH
☐ _____
☐ _____
☐ _____
☐ LOOKING FORWARD

MON   REMEMBER TO REST

TUES

WED

THURS   OBJECTIVELY... HOW ARE YOU?

TODAY MIGHT BE A LITTLE MAGICAL   FRI

YOU AREN'T IN COMPETITION   SAT

IT'S OK TO WONDER   SUN

WEEKLY CHECK-IN: PERSONAL SPACE:
☐ MENTAL HEALTH
☐ PHYSICAL HEALTH
☐ _____
☐ _____
☐ _____
☐ LOOKING FORWARD

MON   I HAVE A GOOD FEELING ABOUT TODAY

TUES

WED

THURS   IT IS HARD BUT YOU CAN DO IT

I'M IN THE PAST, LOVING YOU WHOLEHEARTEDLY   FRI

                                                SAT

NOBODY ELSE WILL MIND   SUN

WEEKLY CHECK-IN: PERSONAL SPACE:
☐ MENTAL HEALTH
☐ PHYSICAL HEALTH
☐ _____
☐ _____
☐ _____
☐ LOOKING FORWARD

MY BIGGEST CHALLENGE LAST MONTH:

A RECURRING THEME:

SOMETHING SPECIAL THAT HAPPENED:

THAT THING I DIDN'T ACTUALLY GET DONE:

GOALS FOR THE MONTH AHEAD:

SOMETHING TO TRY:

DON'T FORGET:

ONE POSITIVE THOUGHT:

THIS IS ACTUALLY

HOW IT WORKS

STEP 1: DRAW YOURSELF AS YOU ARE NOW
STEP 2: DESCRIBE A QUALITY THAT CAN'T BE SEEN

MON   I'M FEELING KIND OF RECKLESS??

TUES   TRUST YOUR PROCESS

WED

THURS

YOU'RE ACTUALLY NOT THAT BAD, LOL   FRI

                                                     SAT

BIG PICTURE? THIS IS FINE   SUN

WEEKLY CHECK-IN: PERSONAL SPACE:

☐ MENTAL HEALTH
☐ PHYSICAL HEALTH
☐ _____
☐ _____
☐ _____
☐ LOOKING FORWARD

MON   WHAT IF WE DON'T DO THAT?

TUES   ASK FOR WHAT YOU'RE WORTH!

WED

THURS   PLEASE GO OUTSIDE

ACKNOWLEDGE YOUR DARKNESS   FRI

                                                             SAT

WHAT'S UP? #NSLCTD   SUN

WEEKLY CHECK-IN: PERSONAL SPACE:
☐ MENTAL HEALTH
☐ PHYSICAL HEALTH
☐ _____
☐ _____
☐ _____
☐ LOOKING FORWARD

NOT ONLY DOES
"PERFECT" NOT
REALLY EXIST
BUT IT'S OFTEN
KIND OF WORSE
IN MANY SITUATIONS
SO FEEL FREE
TO LET THAT
PRESSURE JUST
FLOAT AWAY...

IS IT POSSIBLE YOU COULD
BE FEELING A LITTLE BIT
VULNERABLE LATELY?

LIST 10 PEOPLE NO LONGER
IN YOUR LIFE

1.

2.

3.

4.

5.

6.

7.

8.

9.

10.

IDENTIFY THE FEELING:

[   ]

WHAT IT'S DOING TO YOU:

WHERE IT'S COMING FROM:

IS IT RATIONAL?
☐ YES ☐ NO ☐ KIND OF

CAN YOU HANDLE IT?
☐ YES ☐ NO ☐ KIND OF

THIS PAGE BEING COVERED IN STICKERS
WOULD MAKE ME SO HAPPY AND I'M
NOT GOING TO BE EMBARRASSED BY
MY OWN BEAUTIFUL SINCERITY.

DRAW SOMEONE YOU LOVE
WITH ~~ALL YOUR HEART~~
YOUR FAVORITE PENCIL:

MON   LET'S RUN AWAY

TUES   ART IS HOW WE COMMUNICATE THE INTANGIBLE

WED

THURS   DON'T FORGET YOURSELF

IT'S TIIIIIIIIIIIIME!!!   FRI

                                                            SAT

WE BOTH KNOW YOU DESERVE BETTER   SUN

WEEKLY CHECK-IN: PERSONAL SPACE:
☐ MENTAL HEALTH
☐ PHYSICAL HEALTH
☐ _____
☐ _____
☐ _____
☐ LOOKING FORWARD

MON   LET'S PRETEND THAT DIDN'T HAPPEN

TUES

WED

THURS   YES IT'S HARD... SO WHAT?

YOU DON'T KNOW EVERYTHING   FRI

                                                              SAT

THANK YOU FOR CHECKING IN TODAY   SUN

WEEKLY CHECK-IN: PERSONAL SPACE:
☐ MENTAL HEALTH
☐ PHYSICAL HEALTH
☐ _____
☐ _____
☐ _____
☐ LOOKING FORWARD

MON   IT HELPS TO KNOW YOUR AUDIENCE

TUES   GIVE YOURSELF A CHANCE

WED

THURS

TRY AGAIN TOMORROW   FRI

                                                      SAT

IT'S OKAY TO CANCEL   SUN

WEEKLY CHECK-IN: PERSONAL SPACE:
☐ MENTAL HEALTH
☐ PHYSICAL HEALTH
☐ _____
☐ _____
☐ _____
☐ LOOKING FORWARD

MY BIGGEST CHALLENGE LAST MONTH:

A RECURRING THEME:

SOMETHING SPECIAL THAT HAPPENED:

THAT THING I DIDN'T ACTUALLY GET DONE:

GOALS FOR THE MONTH AHEAD:

SOMETHING TO TRY:

DON'T FORGET:

ONE POSITIVE THOUGHT:

IT'S OKAY AND
EVEN HEALTHY

TO WANT MORE
FOR YOURSELF

WHAT'S SOMETHING REALLY WEIGHING ON YOUR MIND LATELY? HOW HAVE YOU BEEN TAKING CARE OF THE SITUATION?

MON   PROTECT YOUR INVESTMENTS

TUES

WED   YOU ARE ALIVE !!! STILL !!

THURS

RAISE EACH OTHER UP   FRI

                                                       SAT

YOU'RE ENTITLED TO YOUR FEELINGS   SUN

WEEKLY CHECK-IN: PERSONAL SPACE:
☐ MENTAL HEALTH
☐ PHYSICAL HEALTH
☐ _____
☐ _____
☐ _____
☐ LOOKING FORWARD

MON   REWARD YOURSELF FOR TRYING

TUES   ONLY YOU CAN DECIDE

WED   IT'S OK TO BE SENTIMENTAL

THURS

THINGS ARE SHOCKINGLY POSSIBLE   FRI

SAT

CONTROL IS AN ILLUSION   SUN

WEEKLY CHECK-IN: PERSONAL SPACE:
☐ MENTAL HEALTH
☐ PHYSICAL HEALTH
☐ _____
☐ _____
☐ _____
☐ LOOKING FORWARD

NO AMOUNT OF HATING
YOURSELF WILL MAKE
LIFE ANY EASIER???
THIS ONE IS HARD FOR
ME SOMETIMES. CAN
WE JUST AGREE THAT
HATE IS A STRONG
EMOTION WE DON'T
DESERVE TO FEEL FOR
OURSELVES, EVEN IF
WE AREN'T PERFECT?

QUICK, YOU BETTER TAKE ONE

YOU ARE NOT A MIND READER

LOVE IS EVERYTHING

THINGS ARE SHOCKINGLY POSSIBLE

IT IS YOU THOUGH

EVERYTHING IS EVERYTHING

LYING ONLY WORKS A LITTLE

CALM DOWN OH MY GOD

NOTHING IS ANYTHING

NOTHING IS EVERYTHING

HAPPY TO BE HERE

WRITE A REMINDER AS MANY
TIMES AS YOU NEED TO FOR
THE WORDS TO TAKE HOLD:

LIST 10 QUALITIES YOU VALUE

1.

2.

3.

4.

5.

6.

7.

8.

9.

10.

MON

TUES   WHAT IS "WEIRD" EVEN?

WED

THURS   YOU DESERVE BETTER

YOU CAN'T RESTART, BUT YOU CAN PIVOT   FRI

SAT

BEING LOUDER DOESN'T MAKE YOU RIGHT   SUN

WEEKLY CHECK-IN: PERSONAL SPACE:
☐ MENTAL HEALTH
☐ PHYSICAL HEALTH
☐ _____
☐ _____
☐ _____
☐ LOOKING FORWARD

MON

TUES   WHAT DO YOU EVEN WANT?

WED   THIS SEEMS LIKE... GOOD?

THURS

SO WHAT IF YOU FAIL THIS TIME?   FRI

                                                  SAT

CREATE SPACE FOR YOURSELF   SUN

WEEKLY CHECK-IN: PERSONAL SPACE:
☐ MENTAL HEALTH
☐ PHYSICAL HEALTH
☐ _____
☐ _____
☐ _____
☐ LOOKING FORWARD

MON   WHO WILL YOU BE IN A YEAR?

TUES   HOW CAN YOU PRESERVE SPACE FOR OTHERS?

WED

THURS   WHAT'S FOR DINNER? #NSLCTD

THE "HUSTLE" IS EXHAUSTING   FRI

                                                    SAT

THERE'S ONLY FORWARD   SUN

WEEKLY CHECK-IN: PERSONAL SPACE:
☐ MENTAL HEALTH
☐ PHYSICAL HEALTH
☐ _____
☐ _____
☐ _____
☐ LOOKING FORWARD

MY BIGGEST CHALLENGE LAST MONTH:

A RECURRING THEME:

SOMETHING SPECIAL THAT HAPPENED:

THAT THING I DIDN'T ACTUALLY GET DONE:

GOALS FOR THE MONTH AHEAD:

SOMETHING TO TRY:

DON'T FORGET:

ONE POSITIVE THOUGHT:

TIME ACTUALLY
HEALS MANY
WOUNDS

BUT YOU CAN
HELP IT ALONG

STEP 1: DRAW YOUR BAG
STEP 2: DESCRIBE WHAT'S INSIDE

MON   JUST BEING HERE COUNTS

TUES

WED   BE YOUR OWN ADVOCATE

THURS

NEVER GIVING UP IS HOW YOU WIN   FRI

LET GO BEFORE IT CONSUMES YOU   SAT

                                                     SUN

WEEKLY CHECK-IN: PERSONAL SPACE:

☐ MENTAL HEALTH
☐ PHYSICAL HEALTH
☐ _____
☐ _____
☐ _____
☐ LOOKING FORWARD

MON   DO WHATEVER YOU WANT

TUES

WED

THURS   IS THAT BEHAVIOR REALLY HELPING?

THINGS ARE WHAT YOU MAKE OF THEM   FRI

CALL A FRIEND   SAT

                                          SUN

WEEKLY CHECK-IN: PERSONAL SPACE:
☐ MENTAL HEALTH
☐ PHYSICAL HEALTH
☐ _____
☐ _____
☐ _____
☐ LOOKING FORWARD

SO MUCH CHANGES SO
QUICKLY AND THERE'S
OFTEN NOTHING TO DO
BUT GET ON BOARD AND
ADAPT. WITH THIS IN
MIND WHAT IF WE CAN
REFRAME FEELING
"STAGNANT" OR LIKE
YOU "COULD BE DOING
MORE" AS STABILITY
AND TRY TO ENJOY IT?

HOW ARE YOU FEELING TODAY?

RATE YOURSELF ON THE SMILEY SCALE
☺ GOOD   😐 OKAY   ☹ NOT SO MUCH

○ GENERAL OUTLOOK   ○ PERSONAL GROWTH   ○ PHYSICAL HEALTH

○ PLANNING AHEAD   ○ TAKING CARE   ○ EATING WELL

○ SLEEPING HABITS   ○ BEING AWESOME   ○ MENTAL HEALTH

○ CREATIVE THINKING   ○ SHOWING KINDNESS   ○ CALLING FAMILY

○ WORKING HARD   ○ HAVING FUN   ○ BEING A FRIEND

○ STAYING CALM   ○ TRYING HARD   ○ ENJOYING SPACE

○ EARNING INCOME   ○ GOING OUTSIDE   ○ THAT 1 THING

○ FEELING CONTENT   ○ MAKING CONTENT   ○ FIGURING IT OUT

LIST 10 REASONS TO BE PROUD

1.

2.

3.

4.

5.

6.

7.

8.

9.

10.

WHY AM I ENGAGING IN THIS BEHAVIOR AGAIN?

- ☐ BORED
- ☐ "BORED"
- ☐ AVOIDING SOMETHING
- ☐ AFRAID OF ?? IDK?
- ☐ WANT ATTENTION
- ☐ HATE MYSELF A BIT
- ☐ DIDN'T REALIZE IT
- ☐ COULDN'T RESIST
- ☐ I "DESERVE" THIS
- ☐ _____

YOU DON'T HAVE
TO CARRY THAT!

HERE, JUST PUT IT
DOWN FOR A FEW
MINUTES AND REST

I FEEL LIKE YOU MIGHT
WANT TO GET SOMETHING
OFF YOUR MIND AND ONTO
THIS PAGE:

MON   YOU ARE A HUMAN BEING

TUES

WED

THURS   YOU DON'T NEED TO BE POPULAR

YOU DON'T HAVE TO SHARE EVERYTHING   FRI

IT'S ALREADY HAPPENING   SAT

                                                      SUN

WEEKLY CHECK-IN: PERSONAL SPACE:
☐ MENTAL HEALTH
☐ PHYSICAL HEALTH
☐ _____
☐ _____
☐ _____
☐ LOOKING FORWARD

MON   FIND YOUR PLACE (IT'S OUT THERE)

TUES   HAVE A NICE DREAM

WED

THURS

SOME THINGS ARE FREE   FRI

                                                        SAT

I'M NOT SO CONVINCED   SUN

WEEKLY CHECK-IN: PERSONAL SPACE:
☐ MENTAL HEALTH
☐ PHYSICAL HEALTH
☐ _____
☐ _____
☐ _____
☐ LOOKING FORWARD

MON   IMAGINE YOURSELF WITH WHAT YOU THINK YOU WANT

TUES

WED   LOVE IS EVERYWHERE

THURS

REST IS NECESSARY   FRI

THIS IS JUST PAPER... MAKE IT COUNT   SAT

                                                     SUN

WEEKLY CHECK-IN: PERSONAL SPACE:
☐ MENTAL HEALTH
☐ PHYSICAL HEALTH
☐ _____
☐ _____
☐ _____
☐ LOOKING FORWARD

MY BIGGEST CHALLENGE LAST MONTH:

A RECURRING THEME:

SOMETHING SPECIAL THAT HAPPENED:

THAT THING I DIDN'T ACTUALLY GET DONE:

GOALS FOR THE MONTH AHEAD:

SOMETHING TO TRY:

DON'T FORGET:

ONE POSITIVE THOUGHT:

IS THERE A RELATIONSHIP IN YOUR LIFE
THAT'S NOT FEELING RIGHT? ARE YOU
ABLE TO HAVE AN OPEN CONVERSATION
TOGETHER TO EITHER REPAIR OR MOVE ON?

CONNECT THE DOTS IN ANY ORDER:

WHAT DO YOU SEE: _____

MON

TUES   SUNSHINE DOES HELP

WED   BUT MAYBE... YES?

THURS

BREATHE IN. BREATHE OUT. REPEAT.   FRI

                                                    SAT

YOU HAVE THE CAPACITY TO LEARN NEW THINGS   SUN

WEEKLY CHECK-IN: PERSONAL SPACE:
☐ MENTAL HEALTH
☐ PHYSICAL HEALTH
☐ _____
☐ _____
☐ _____
☐ LOOKING FORWARD

MON   IT'S MORE FUN WHEN YOU STOP TRYING TO CONTROL IT

TUES

WED   IT'S OK TO CRY

THURS

OF COURSE YOU'RE GOOD ENOUGH   FRI

SAT

TODAY IS ENTIRELY UP TO YOU   SUN

WEEKLY CHECK-IN: PERSONAL SPACE:

☐ MENTAL HEALTH
☐ PHYSICAL HEALTH
☐ _____
☐ _____
☐ _____
☐ LOOKING FORWARD

BRAIN OVERHEATED?
HAVE YOU TRIED
UNPLUGGING FOR
FIVE MINUTES AND
THEN PLUGGING
BACK IN AGAIN?
YOU'D BE SURPRISED
HOW OFTEN THIS
ACTUALLY WORKS.

IF YOU'VE BEEN CARRYING AROUND AN
ANCIENT SCRAP OF PAPER IN YOUR BAG
OR WALLET OR A SPECIFIC COAT, TODAY
IS THE DAY TO TAPE IT IN HERE AND SET
THIS ONE FREE...

LIST 10 THINGS THAT MADE YOU HAPPY RECENTLY

1.

2.

3.

4.

5.

6.

7.

8.

9.

10.

WE INTERRUPT THIS PLANNER
FOR A BREAKING NEWS UPDATE:

THE YEAR IS HALF OVER
AND YOU'RE STILL ALIVE !!!

MON   IT'S NOT HELPING UNLESS IT HELPS

TUES

WED

THURS   IN HERE THERE ARE NO WRONG ANSWERS

THIS IS JUST PAPER   FRI

                                                               SAT

YOU ARE HERE *FOR NOW   SUN

WEEKLY CHECK-IN: PERSONAL SPACE:
☐ MENTAL HEALTH
☐ PHYSICAL HEALTH
☐ _____
☐ _____
☐ _____
☐ LOOKING FORWARD

MON   WHAT IF YOU ASK MORE QUESTIONS?

TUES

WED

THURS   WHAT IF... NOT THAT?

FRI

CREATE A PERIMETER   SAT

(NOTHING TO SEE HERE)   SUN

WEEKLY CHECK-IN: PERSONAL SPACE:
☐ MENTAL HEALTH
☐ PHYSICAL HEALTH
☐ _____
☐ _____
☐ _____
☐ LOOKING FORWARD

MON   MAYBE EAT SOME NUTRIENTS

TUES

WED

THURS   WHAT IF WE HIT PAUSE ON THAT ONE INSECURITY?

DELETE YOUR ACCOUNT   FRI

                                                       SAT

LET'S GET REALLY REALLY REAL   SUN

WEEKLY CHECK-IN: PERSONAL SPACE:
☐ MENTAL HEALTH
☐ PHYSICAL HEALTH
☐ _____
☐ _____
☐ _____
☐ LOOKING FORWARD

MY BIGGEST CHALLENGE LAST MONTH:

A RECURRING THEME:

SOMETHING SPECIAL THAT HAPPENED:

THAT THING I DIDN'T ACTUALLY GET DONE:

GOALS FOR THE MONTH AHEAD:

SOMETHING TO TRY:

DON'T FORGET:

ONE POSITIVE THOUGHT:

PICK <u>ONE</u> CONCERN TO FOCUS ON
AND LET'S TRY TO BREAK IT DOWN

FIRST, THE THING

THEN, WHAT IT FEELS LIKE

NEXT, WHAT YOU KNOW AS FACT

NOW, WHAT REQUIRES PATIENCE

STEP 1: DRAW A FAMILY PORTRAIT
STEP 2: DESCRIBE WHAT THEY MEAN TO YOU

MON   I'M GRATEFUL YOU EXIST

TUES

WED

THURS   THINK ABOUT IT

JUST WAIT A MINUTE   FRI

YOU BELONG (MAYBE HERE)   SAT

                                                      SUN

WEEKLY CHECK-IN: PERSONAL SPACE:
☐ MENTAL HEALTH
☐ PHYSICAL HEALTH
☐ _____
☐ _____
☐ _____
☐ LOOKING FORWARD

MON   YOU ARE PART OF A COMMUNITY

TUES   HAVE NEW EXPERIENCES

WED

THURS

TAKE A NAP   FRI

                                                              SAT

IT'S OK TO LAUGH   SUN

WEEKLY CHECK-IN: PERSONAL SPACE:
☐ MENTAL HEALTH
☐ PHYSICAL HEALTH
☐ _____
☐ _____
☐ _____
☐ LOOKING FORWARD

DO WHAT YOU LOVE
AND YOU'LL ~~NEVER~~
WORK ~~A DAY IN YOUR~~
~~LIFE~~ SUPER HARD
ALL THE TIME WITH
NO SEPARATION OR
ANY BOUNDARIES
AND ALSO TAKE
EVERYTHING EX-
TREMELY PERSONALLY.

TAPE $5 TO THIS PAGE AND
TRY TO FORGET ABOUT IT.

LIST 10 THINGS YOU'VE LEARNED THIS YEAR

1.

2.

3.

4.

5.

6.

7.

8.

9.

10.

DISGUISE YOUR TRUE FEELINGS
BY WRAPPING THEM IN OTHER
EMOTIONS AND/OR EXCUSES:

MON   IT'S (ALMOST) NEVER TOO LATE

TUES

WED   IT'S NOT YOUR JOB TO WORRY

THURS

IDK BUT I DO LOVE YOU   FRI

                                                          SAT

FRIENDSHIPS SHIFT BUT THE MEMORIES MATTER   SUN

WEEKLY CHECK-IN: PERSONAL SPACE:
☐ MENTAL HEALTH
☐ PHYSICAL HEALTH
☐ _____
☐ _____
☐ _____
☐ LOOKING FORWARD

MON   MAKE YOUR PRIORITIES A PRIORITY

TUES   GO BE ALONE

WED

THURS

BE KIND ALWAYS   FRI

                                                  SAT

HOW DO YOU KNOW THAT?   SUN

WEEKLY CHECK-IN: PERSONAL SPACE:
☐ MENTAL HEALTH
☐ PHYSICAL HEALTH
☐ _____
☐ _____
☐ _____
☐ LOOKING FORWARD

MON   LET YOURSELF BE

TUES

WED

THURS   IT WILL BE HARD SOMETIMES

ENJOY THE UNKNOWN   FRI

                                                     SAT

TIME TO REALLY CHOOSE   SUN

WEEKLY CHECK-IN: PERSONAL SPACE:
☐ MENTAL HEALTH
☐ PHYSICAL HEALTH
☐ _____
☐ _____
☐ _____
☐ LOOKING FORWARD

MY BIGGEST CHALLENGE LAST MONTH:

A RECURRING THEME:

SOMETHING SPECIAL THAT HAPPENED:

THAT THING I DIDN'T ACTUALLY GET DONE:

GOALS FOR THE MONTH AHEAD:

SOMETHING TO TRY:

DON'T FORGET:

ONE POSITIVE THOUGHT:

FIVE MINUTES OF
TUNNEL VISION

FOR ONE SINGLE
POTENTIAL FUTURE

HOW IS YOUR PHYSICAL SELF THESE DAYS? HOW IS YOUR CLOTHING HAVING AN IMPACT? DO YOU FEEL STRONG? WHAT ARE YOU DOING FOR ANY PAIN?

MON   YOU WERE BORN (SORRY NO TAKE-BACKS)

TUES

WED   UHH ARE YOU SURE THOUGH?

THURS

SOME THINGS ARE UNCERTAIN   FRI

TAKE A BREAK   SAT

                                                   SUN

WEEKLY CHECK-IN: PERSONAL SPACE:
☐ MENTAL HEALTH
☐ PHYSICAL HEALTH
☐ _____
☐ _____
☐ _____
☐ LOOKING FORWARD

MON

TUES   GO TO SLEEP

WED   LISTEN, I'M SCARED TOO

THURS

YOU ARE HERE IN TIME AND SPACE (OMFG)   FRI

                                                SAT

YOU MIGHT NOT WANT TO, BUT YOU CAN   SUN

WEEKLY CHECK-IN: PERSONAL SPACE:
☐ MENTAL HEALTH
☐ PHYSICAL HEALTH
☐ _____
☐ _____
☐ _____
☐ LOOKING FORWARD

WE ARE CONNECTED
BY A CHOICE TO
BE HERE RIGHT NOW
AND THEN AND SOON
AND AGAIN ON THIS
PAGE IN THESE WORDS
WITHIN THIS THOUGHT
AND THERE IS A
KIND OF POWER HERE
IN THIS MOMENT.

HOW ARE YOU FEELING TODAY?

RATE YOURSELF ON THE SMILEY SCALE
☺ GOOD   😐 OKAY   ☹ NOT SO MUCH

○ GENERAL OUTLOOK   ○ PERSONAL GROWTH   ○ PHYSICAL HEALTH

○ PLANNING AHEAD   ○ TAKING CARE   ○ EATING WELL

○ SLEEPING HABITS   ○ BEING AWESOME   ○ MENTAL HEALTH

○ CREATIVE THINKING   ○ SHOWING KINDNESS   ○ CALLING FAMILY

○ WORKING HARD   ○ HAVING FUN   ○ BEING A FRIEND

○ STAYING CALM   ○ TRYING HARD   ○ ENJOYING SPACE

○ EARNING INCOME   ○ GOING OUTSIDE   ○ THAT 1 THING

○ FEELING CONTENT   ○ MAKING CONTENT   ○ FIGURING IT OUT

LIST 10 IRRATIONAL FEARS YOU JUST CAN'T LET GO OF

1.

2.

3.

4.

5.

6.

7. EVERYONE HATES ME SECRETLY

8.

9.

10.

WHATEVER THAT THING IS, JUST
WRITE IT IN HERE AND PLEASE
TURN THE PAGE OKAY THANKS!

MON   LET'S JUST WORRY ABOUT THAT LATER

TUES

WED   THE WORLD MIGHT BE ENDING BUT YOU STILL NEED REST

THURS

HERE WE GO AGAIN   FRI

IT CAN BE LIBERATING TO TRY   SAT

                                                    SUN

WEEKLY CHECK-IN: PERSONAL SPACE:
☐ MENTAL HEALTH
☐ PHYSICAL HEALTH
☐ _____
☐ _____
☐ _____
☐ LOOKING FORWARD

MON   GO OUTSIDE

TUES

WED   YOU ARE LITERALLY POWERFUL

THURS

SELF-CONFIDENCE PLEASE!!   FRI

LIFE IS SURPRISING BUT PATTERNS FORM   SAT

                                                  SUN

WEEKLY CHECK-IN: PERSONAL SPACE:
☐ MENTAL HEALTH
☐ PHYSICAL HEALTH
☐ _____
☐ _____
☐ _____
☐ LOOKING FORWARD

MON   EVERYTHING ENDS EVENTUALLY (BUT NOT YET)

TUES

WED   YOU ARE ACTUALLY STRONG THOUGH

THURS

GET SOME REST   FRI

                                                 SAT

TRUST IS ABSOLUTELY CRUCIAL   SUN

WEEKLY CHECK-IN: PERSONAL SPACE:
☐ MENTAL HEALTH
☐ PHYSICAL HEALTH
☐ _____
☐ _____
☐ _____
☐ LOOKING FORWARD

MY BIGGEST CHALLENGE LAST MONTH:

A RECURRING THEME:

SOMETHING SPECIAL THAT HAPPENED:

THAT THING I DIDN'T ACTUALLY GET DONE:

GOALS FOR THE MONTH AHEAD:

SOMETHING TO TRY:

DON'T FORGET:

ONE POSITIVE THOUGHT:

HONESTLY
SURPRISED

TO STILL
BE ALIVE

STEP 1: DRAW ~~YOUR HOME~~ WHERE YOU LIVE
STEP 2: EXPLAIN WHAT MAKES IT HOME

MON

WASH YOUR FACE

TUES

HOW'S IT GOING? #NSLCTD

WED

THURS

SIMPLE CHANGES CAN ADD UP

THAT FEELING MIGHT HAVE A POINT   FRI

                                                          SAT

MAYBE IT'S NOT A 2 COFFEE DAY   SUN

WEEKLY CHECK-IN: PERSONAL SPACE:
☐ MENTAL HEALTH
☐ PHYSICAL HEALTH
☐ _____
☐ _____
☐ _____
☐ LOOKING FORWARD

MON   WHAT DO YOU THINK WILL HAPPEN NEXT?

TUES

WED   LET'S BOTH BREATHE

THURS

I'M DOING THIS ~~FOR YOU~~ ~~FOR US~~ FOREVER   FRI

FIND YOUR PEOPLE   SAT

                                                                 SUN

WEEKLY CHECK-IN: PERSONAL SPACE:
☐ MENTAL HEALTH
☐ PHYSICAL HEALTH
☐ _____
☐ _____
☐ _____
☐ LOOKING FORWARD

AT A CERTAIN POINT
YOU ACTUALLY JUST
HAVE TO CHOOSE
AND SO THE QUESTION
BECOMES CLEAR:

WHO ARE YOU AND
WHAT DO YOU
REALLY WANT?

CREATE A PLAN.

PRINT OUT YOUR FAVORITE PHOTO OF
YOURSELF FROM THE LAST SIX MONTHS.
WHAT DO YOU LOVE ABOUT THIS PHOTO?

LIST 10 PLACES YOU'VE BEEN LATELY

1.

2.

3.

4.

5.

6.

7.

8.

9.

10.

TAPE A POSTCARD
TO THIS PAGE

MON   IT'S OK TO BE OPEN

TUES

WED

THURS   PRETENDING CAN ONLY WORK SO WELL

YOU NEED TO GET OUT   FRI

FOCUS ON THE PEOPLE WHO CARE   SAT

                                                                       SUN

WEEKLY CHECK-IN: PERSONAL SPACE:

☐ MENTAL HEALTH
☐ PHYSICAL HEALTH
☐ _____
☐ _____
☐ _____
☐ LOOKING FORWARD

MON   LOOK AHEAD IF YOU CAN

TUES

WED

THURS   NOBODY NOTICED, IT'S OK

IF LOVE IS REAL, WHAT ELSE MIGHT BE REAL???   FRI

SAT

ASK YOURSELF THE QUESTIONS   SUN

WEEKLY CHECK-IN: PERSONAL SPACE:

☐ MENTAL HEALTH
☐ PHYSICAL HEALTH
☐ _____
☐ _____
☐ _____
☐ LOOKING FORWARD

MON   BREATHE DEEP

TUES

WED

THURS   PLEASE PLEASE JUST BELIEVE

THINGS DO CHANGE   FRI

PROCEED WITH CAUTION   SAT

PEOPLE CHOOSE TO CARE   SUN

WEEKLY CHECK-IN: PERSONAL SPACE:
☐ MENTAL HEALTH
☐ PHYSICAL HEALTH
☐ _____
☐ _____
☐ _____
☐ LOOKING FORWARD

MY BIGGEST CHALLENGE LAST MONTH:

A RECURRING THEME:

SOMETHING SPECIAL THAT HAPPENED:

THAT THING I DIDN'T ACTUALLY GET DONE:

GOALS FOR THE MONTH AHEAD:

SOMETHING TO TRY:

DON'T FORGET:

ONE POSITIVE THOUGHT:

WHEN WAS THE LAST TIME YOU HAD
A TRULY "PERFECT" DAY? WHAT OR
WHO MADE THE DAY SO SPECIAL?

DRAW SIX THINGS NEAR YOU

MON   TREAT YOURSELF WITH RESPECT

TUES   IN CASE YOU MISSED IT: YESTERDAY!

WED

THURS

THERE HAS TO BE MORE   FRI

                                                        SAT

CLOSE YOUR EYES FOR A MOMENT AND BREATHE   SUN

WEEKLY CHECK-IN: PERSONAL SPACE:
☐ MENTAL HEALTH
☐ PHYSICAL HEALTH
☐ _____
☐ _____
☐ _____
☐ LOOKING FORWARD

MON   EAT SOME GREENS

TUES   ASK FOR ASSISTANCE

WED

THURS

FAILURE ACTUALLY IS AN OPTION   FRI

                                                  SAT

HAPPINESS IS AN ART   SUN

WEEKLY CHECK-IN: PERSONAL SPACE:
☐ MENTAL HEALTH
☐ PHYSICAL HEALTH
☐ _____
☐ _____
☐ _____
☐ LOOKING FORWARD

IF YOU'RE SOMEONE
WHO LOVES YOUR
FRIENDS AND KNOWS
THEY CAN DO ANY-
THING AND IS GOOD
AT ENCOURAGING
THEM... HAVE YOU
TRIED DOING THAT
FOR YOURSELF TOO?

HOW ARE YOU FEELING TODAY?

RATE YOURSELF ON THE SMILEY SCALE
☺ GOOD ☺ OKAY ☹ NOT SO MUCH

- ○ GENERAL OUTLOOK
- ○ PERSONAL GROWTH
- ○ PHYSICAL HEALTH
- ○ PLANNING AHEAD
- ○ TAKING CARE
- ○ EATING WELL
- ○ SLEEPING HABITS
- ○ BEING AWESOME
- ○ MENTAL HEALTH
- ○ CREATIVE THINKING
- ○ SHOWING KINDNESS
- ○ CALLING FAMILY
- ○ WORKING HARD
- ○ HAVING FUN
- ○ BEING A FRIEND
- ○ STAYING CALM
- ○ TRYING HARD
- ○ ENJOYING SPACE
- ○ EARNING INCOME
- ○ GOING OUTSIDE
- ○ THAT 1 THING
- ○ FEELING CONTENT
- ○ MAKING CONTENT
- ○ FIGURING IT OUT

LIST 10 BOOKS/FILMS/ETC. THAT YOU LIKED RECENTLY

1.

2.

3.

4.

5.

6.

7.

8.

9.

10.

WRITE SOMETHING TOO HONEST AND EITHER
SAVE IT FOREVER OR IMMEDIATELY TEAR IT OUT

EMERGENCY EXIT:

USE IN CASE OF
NON-LINEAR MEMORY

FEELING OUT OF YOUR MIND?
TRYING TO FIND A PROFOUND
EXPERIENCE IN THE MADNESS?
LET'S PROCESS, BABY:

MON

GIVE YOURSELF A REAL CHANCE

TUES

INHALE, EXHALE

WED

THURS

SOME PEOPLE JUST WON'T LIKE YOU

YOU STILL HAVE TO SHOW UP   FRI

SAT

THINGS ARE MOSTLY FINE   SUN

WEEKLY CHECK-IN: PERSONAL SPACE:

☐ MENTAL HEALTH
☐ PHYSICAL HEALTH
☐ _____
☐ _____
☐ _____
☐ LOOKING FORWARD

MON   SEE YOU NEXT TIME

TUES   YOU'RE NOT REALLY ALONE

WED

THURS   WAIT IS THERE A BIRTHDAY COMING UP??

TGIF (THANK GOD I FORGOT)   FRI

                                                       SAT

ANYTHING CAN BE A MIRACLE   SUN

WEEKLY CHECK-IN: PERSONAL SPACE:
☐ MENTAL HEALTH
☐ PHYSICAL HEALTH
☐ _____
☐ _____
☐ _____
☐ LOOKING FORWARD

MON   WE ALL LOVE YOU VERY MUCH

TUES

WED

THURS   FIND YOUR WAY BACK

TRY REACHING OUT   FRI

YOU'RE SOMEBODY'S WORLD   SAT

                                           SUN

WEEKLY CHECK-IN: PERSONAL SPACE:
☐ MENTAL HEALTH
☐ PHYSICAL HEALTH
☐ _____
☐ _____
☐ _____
☐ LOOKING FORWARD

MY BIGGEST CHALLENGE LAST MONTH:

A RECURRING THEME:

SOMETHING SPECIAL THAT HAPPENED:

THAT THING I DIDN'T ACTUALLY GET DONE:

GOALS FOR THE MONTH AHEAD:

SOMETHING TO TRY:

DON'T FORGET:

ONE POSITIVE THOUGHT:

IF YOU FEEL LIKE
YOU NEED TO SCREAM
THAT'S OK BUT TRY
TO KEEP IT INSIDE
THIS CIRCLE PLEASE:

SAFETY
ZONE

STEP 1: DRAW YOUR PHONE
STEP 2: DESCRIBE HOW IT MAKES YOU FEEL

MON

ALWAYS
FEELINGS AREN'T RATIONAL BUT
YOU STILL HAVE TO FEEL THEM

TUES

EMBRACE BREATHING

WED

THURS

WE ARE BOTH RIGHT HERE

FRI

SAT

SUNLIGHT DOES HELP   SUN

WEEKLY CHECK-IN: PERSONAL SPACE:
☐ MENTAL HEALTH
☐ PHYSICAL HEALTH
☐ _____
☐ _____
☐ _____
☐ LOOKING FORWARD

MON   THERE MAY NOT BE AN EASIER WAY

TUES   IT DOES SEEM POSSIBLE

WED

THURS

EVERYONE GETS SAD   FRI

                                                     SAT

START A NEW BOOK THIS WEEK   SUN

WEEKLY CHECK-IN: PERSONAL SPACE:
☐ MENTAL HEALTH
☐ PHYSICAL HEALTH
☐ _____
☐ _____
☐ _____
☐ LOOKING FORWARD

IT'S VERY ANNOYING
BUT THE ONLY PERSON
YOU CAN ACTUALLY
CHANGE IS YOURSELF!

THE GOOD NEWS IS
THAT IT'S A FULL-
TIME JOB ANYWAY
SO IF YOU'RE TRULY
FOCUSED YOU'LL BE
TOO BUSY TO WORRY
ABOUT ANYONE ELSE.

YOU KNOW THAT COOL PEN YOU BOUGHT
THAT NEVER GETS USED? WHAT IF YOU
JUST SCRIBBLED HERE WITH THAT ONE!?

IF YOU TAKE A MINUTE TO THINK WITHOUT A JOKE OR DISTRACTION, HOW IS YOUR MENTAL HEALTH ACTUALLY? WHAT FACTORS MIGHT BE MAKING AN IMPACT LATELY?

PICK ONE CONCERN TO FOCUS ON
AND LET'S TRY TO BREAK IT DOWN

FIRST, THE THING

THEN, WHAT IT FEELS LIKE

NEXT, WHAT YOU KNOW AS FACT

NOW, WHAT REQUIRES PATIENCE

MON   TAKE SOME TIME

TUES

WED   IT'S NOBODY'S "FAULT"

THURS   HOW DO YOU KNOW WHEN YOU KNOW?

WHAT IF WE JUST DIDN'T?   FRI

MAGIC IS OUT THERE   SAT

                                           SUN

WEEKLY CHECK-IN: PERSONAL SPACE:
☐ MENTAL HEALTH
☐ PHYSICAL HEALTH
☐ _____
☐ _____
☐ _____
☐ LOOKING FORWARD

MON   OK BUT WHAT IF WE DID?

TUES

WED

THURS   KNOWING ISN'T FEELING

WHAT DOES IT FEEL LIKE?   FRI

                                           SAT

MEET BACK HERE TOMORROW?   SUN

WEEKLY CHECK-IN: PERSONAL SPACE:
☐ MENTAL HEALTH
☐ PHYSICAL HEALTH
☐ _____
☐ _____
☐ _____
☐ LOOKING FORWARD

MON   TAKE A MOMENT TO FEEL PROUD

TUES   YOU LOVE TO SEE IT!

WED

THURS

CHECK YOUR HOROSCOPE (JUST IN CASE)   FRI

                                                        SAT

IMAGINE YOUR FUTURE SELF   SUN

WEEKLY CHECK-IN: PERSONAL SPACE:
☐ MENTAL HEALTH
☐ PHYSICAL HEALTH
☐ _____
☐ _____
☐ _____
☐ LOOKING FORWARD

MY BIGGEST CHALLENGE LAST MONTH:

A RECURRING THEME:

SOMETHING SPECIAL THAT HAPPENED:

THAT THING I DIDN'T ACTUALLY GET DONE:

GOALS FOR THE MONTH AHEAD:

SOMETHING TO TRY:

DON'T FORGET:

ONE POSITIVE THOUGHT:

TELL ME ABOUT SOMEONE YOU LOVE:
WHAT HAVE THEY DONE LATELY THAT
MADE YOU HAPPY? HOW DID YOU LET
THEM KNOW WHAT THEY MEAN TO YOU?

STEP 1: DRAW YOUR MOST PRIZED POSSESSION
STEP 2: EXPLAIN WHAT IT MEANS TO YOU

MON   GET OUTTA HERE

TUES   WHERE ARE YOU NOW? #NSLCTD

WED

THURS   JUST HAPPY TO BE HERE

NOBODY EXPECTS YOU TO BE THE BEST   FRI

                                                     SAT

WE GENUINELY DESERVE THIS   SUN

WEEKLY CHECK-IN: PERSONAL SPACE:
☐ MENTAL HEALTH
☐ PHYSICAL HEALTH
☐ _____
☐ _____
☐ _____
☐ LOOKING FORWARD

MON   IT'S OK TO NOT KNOW

TUES

WED

THURS   WAIT... WHAT BIRTHDAY?

EVERYTHING CHANGES   FRI

                                                      SAT

OH WOW THIS AGAIN   SUN

WEEKLY CHECK-IN: PERSONAL SPACE:
☐ MENTAL HEALTH
☐ PHYSICAL HEALTH
☐ _____
☐ _____
☐ _____
☐ LOOKING FORWARD

MON   TAKE SOME TIME TO PREPARE

TUES   SCREW IT — LET'S GO

WED

THURS   PERFECT ISN'T BETTER

GO FOR A WALK   FRI

                                                 SAT

                                                 SUN

WEEKLY CHECK-IN: PERSONAL SPACE:
☐ MENTAL HEALTH
☐ PHYSICAL HEALTH
☐ _____
☐ _____
☐ _____
☐ LOOKING FORWARD

OH YOU THOUGHT
THIS WAS OVER?

WE KEEP GOING

MAKE A PLAN

How will you continue to build on the work you've done here outside of the structure of this particular planner format?

Which parts of this planner felt most useful, and how did they help shape your experience in the past year?

What tools might you replicate for yourself with pencil and paper? What no longer feels necessary?

Who else might benefit from a little *Unsolicited Advice?*

CAN YOU REMEMBER A PARTICULAR
DAY WHEN SOME "UNSOLICITED
ADVICE" ALIGNED ALMOST TOO
PERFECTLY TO NOT MEAN...
SOMETHING?

YOU ARE SPECIAL TO ME (OKAY BYE)

The first *Unsolicited Advice* planner was printed after hours at my copy center job in 2011, and it changed my life, making a creative life possible for me. Whatever your thing is, please please please just try! You never know what might happen.

This forever-ish edition is my way to say "thank you always" without saying goodbye, but we do still have to navigate linear time (womp womp) and end here. But I made some other books and journals that are all in conversation with each other if my inner monologue is a little like yours . . .

Adam J. Kurtz is an artist and author who is trying to make the best of things, one page at a time. His creative books and journals have sold over a million copies worldwide in over a dozen languages, which kind of breaks his brain a little.

WWW.ADAMJK.COM @ADAMJK

UNSOLICITED ADVICE:

- ☐ WASH YOUR HANDS
- ☐ LOOK BOTH WAYS
- ☐ TREAT OTHERS KINDLY
- ☐ EVEN YOURSELF
- ☐ EAT VEGETABLES
- ☐ SMILE AT DOGS
- ☐ FEEL YOUR POWER
- ☐ SHARE YOUR GIFTS
- ☐ FEEL THE SUN
- ☐ TOUCH A FLOWER'S FACE
- ☐ TRY NEW THINGS
- ☐ IT IS POSSIBLE
- ☐ LIFE GOES ON
- ☐ GOOD THINGS HAPPEN
- ☐ LOVE IS REAL
- ☐ WE WILL BE OKAY